C A N A D I A N
B R A S S
SERIES OF
COLLECTED QUINTETS

Exciting repertory books of quintets, containing a wide variety of literature. These easy and intermediate collections retain the flavor of Canadian Brass recorded repertory, and the selection of the music and the arrangements for this series were supervised by the Canadian Brass.

Easy level (1-3 years experience):

Easy Classics
arranged by Charles Sayre
Contents: Two Chorales — O Sacred Head, and Break Forth, O Beauteous Heavenly Light (Bach); Two Fuguing Tunes — When Jesus Wept and Kittery (Billings); Victorious Love (Gastoldi); In the Hall of the Mountain King (Grieg); Austrian Hymn (Haydn); Canon (Tallis).

50488760 Trumpet I
50488761 Trumpet II
50488762 Horn in F
50488763 Trombone
50488764 Tuba
50488765 Conductor's Score

Hymns for Brass
Contents: Ah, Holy Jesus; Beautiful Saviour; Christ the Lord Is Risen Today; Eternal Father, Strong to Save; A Mighty Fortress Is Our God; We Gather Together.

50488754 Trumpet I
50488755 Trumpet II
50488756 Horn in F
50488757 Trombone
50488758 Tuba
50488759 Conductor's Score

Rodgers and Hammerstein Hits
arranged by Charles Sayre
Contents: Edelweiss *(The Sound of Music);* Oklahoma *(Oklahoma);* You'll Never Walk Alone *(Carousel);* Oh, What a Beautiful Morning *(Oklahoma);* Blow High, Blow Low *(Carousel);* Honey Bun *(South Pacific).*

50488766 Trumpet I
50488767 Trumpet II
50488768 Horn in F
50488769 Trombone
50488770 Tuba
50488771 Conductor's Score

Intermediate level (4 years or more playing experience):

Brass on Broadway
arranged by Bob Lowden
Contents: Broadway Baby *(Follies);* Comedy Tonight *(A Funny Thing Happened on the Way to the Forum);* Get Me to the Church on Time *(My Fair Lady);* Ol' Man River *(Show Boat):* Sunrise, Sunset *(Fiddler on the Roof)*

50488778 Trumpet I
50488779 Trumpet II
50488780 Horn in F
50488781 Trombone
50488782 Tuba
50488783 Conductor's Score

Favorite Classics
arranged by Henry Charles Smith
Contents: Gavotte from the Sixth Cello Suite (Bach); Prayer from *Hansel and Gretel* (Humperdinck); Cantate Domino (Pitoni); TheLiberty Bell (Sousa); Questo e quella from Rigoletto (Verdi); Pilgrim's Chorus from *Tannhauser* (Wagner).

50488784 Trumpet I
50488785 Trumpet II
50488786 Horn in F
50488787 Trombone
50488788 Tuba
50488789 Conductor's Score

Immortal Folksongs
arranged by Terry Vosbein
Contents: Greensleeves; High Barbary; Londonderry Air; Shenandoah; Simple Gifts; The Drunken Sailor.

50488772 Trumpet I
50488773 Trumpet II
50488774 Horn in F
50488775 Trombone
50488776 Tuba
50488777 Conductor's Score

CANADIAN BRASS
SERIES OF COLLECTED QUINTETS

HYMNS FOR BRASS

arranged for brass quintet
by Rick Walters

contents

Welcome to the new *Canadian Brass Series of Collected Quintets.* In our work with students we have for some time been aware of the need for more brass quintet music at easy and intermediate levels of difficulty. We are continually observing a kind of "Renaissance" in brass music, not only in audience responses to our quintet, but to all brass music in general. The brass quintet, as a chamber ensemble, seems to have become as standard a chamber combination as a string quartet. That could not have been said twenty-five years ago. Brass quintets are popping up everywhere — professional quintets, junior and senior high school ensembles, college and university groups, and amateur quintets of adult players.

We have carefully chosen the literature for these collected quintets, and closely supervised the arrangements. Our aim was to retain a Canadian Brass flavor to each arrangement, and create attractive repertory designed so that any brass quintet can play it with satisfying results. We've often remarked to one another that we certainly wish that we'd had quintet arrangements like these when we were students!

Happy playing to you and your quintet.

— THE CANADIAN BRASS

HAL•LEONARD®
CORPORATION
7777 W. BLUEMOUND RD P.O. BOX 13819 MILWAUKEE, WI 53213

Ah, Holy Jesus

Johannes Crüger
("Herzliebster Jesu")

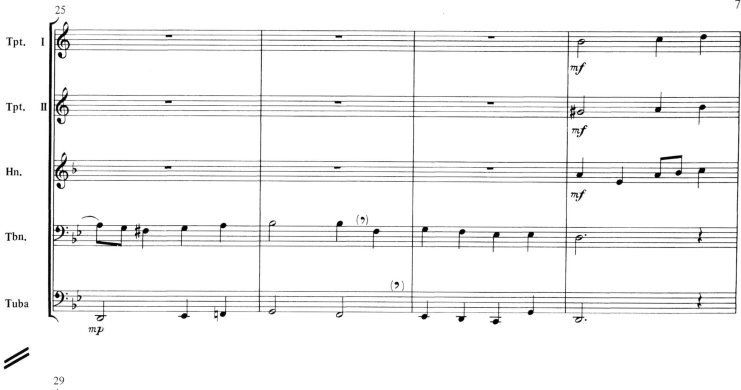

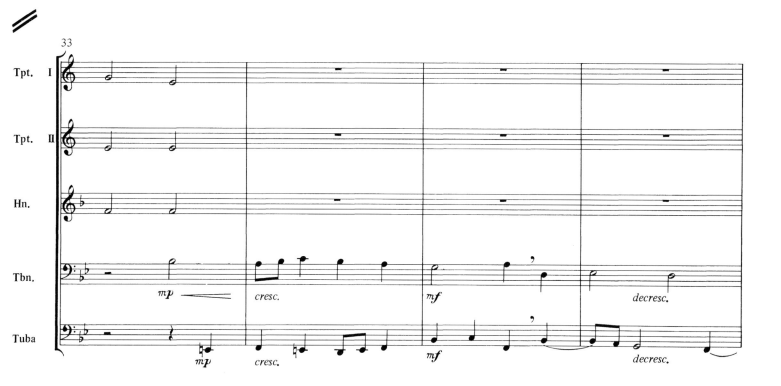

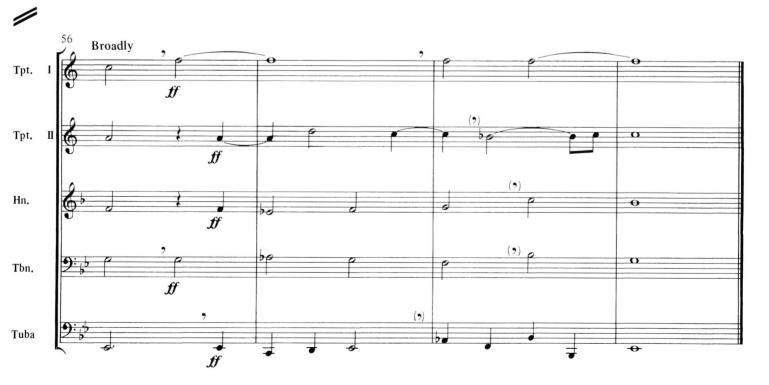

Christ the Lord is Risen Today

from *Lyra Davidica*, 1708

Eternal Father, Strong to Save

John B. Dykes, c. 1861

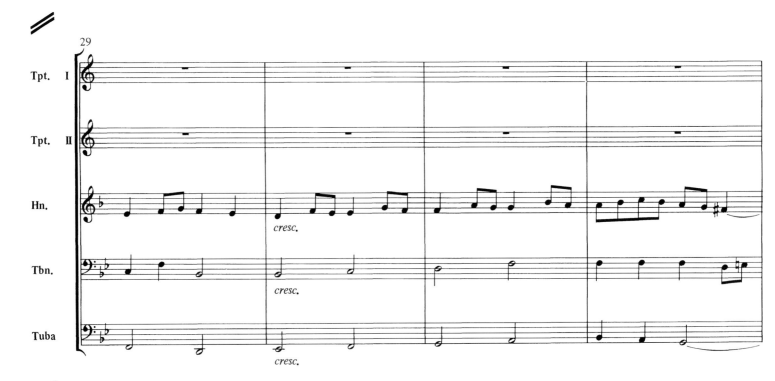

Beautiful Savior

Silesian Melody
(Schönster Herr Jesu)

A Mighty Fortress

Martin Luther, 1529

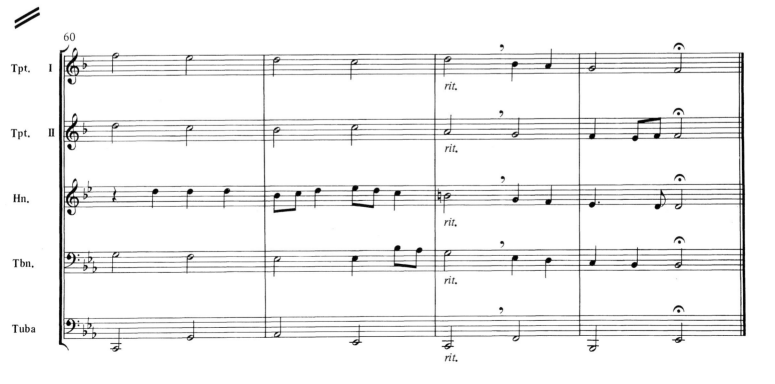

We Gather Together

Netherlands Folk Song, 1626

CONTENTS

Adelaide
Op. 46
By Ludwig van Beethoven

Drop D tuning:
(low to high) D-A-D-G-B-E

Moderately

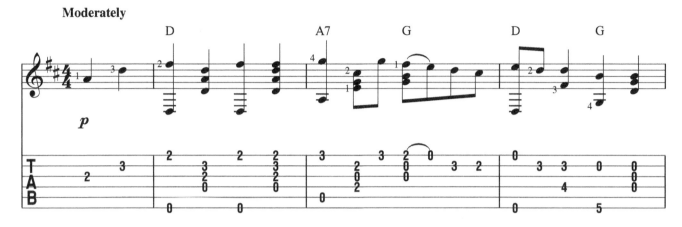

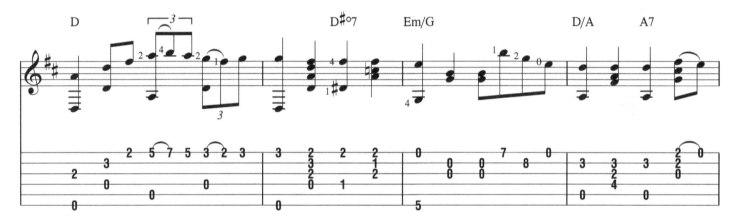

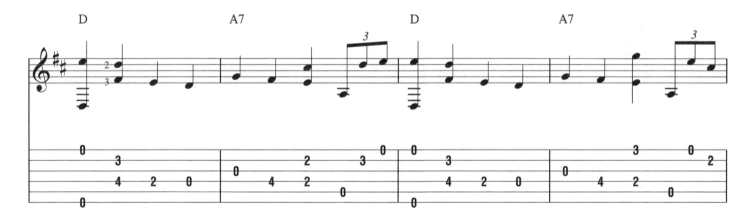

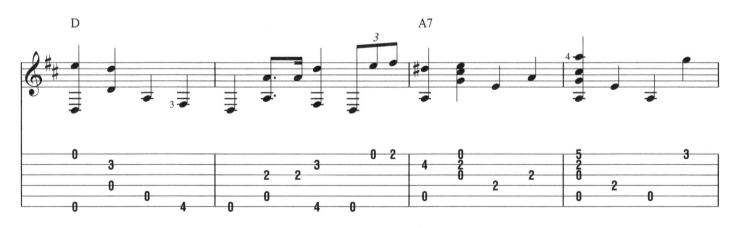

FINGERPICKING
Beethoven

ISBN 978-1-4584-0523-4

HAL•LEONARD®
CORPORATION
7777 W. BLUEMOUND RD. P.O. BOX 13819 MILWAUKEE, WI 53213

In Australia Contact:
Hal Leonard Australia Pty. Ltd.
4 Lentara Court
Cheltenham, Victoria, 3192 Australia
Email: ausadmin@halleonard.com.au

Visit Hal Leonard Online at
www.halleonard.com

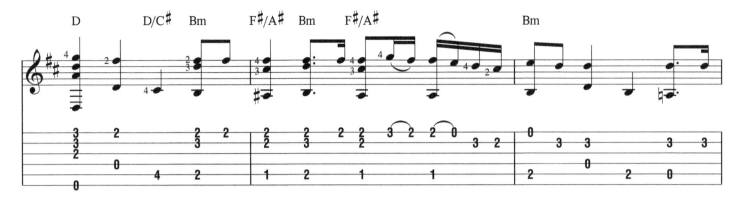

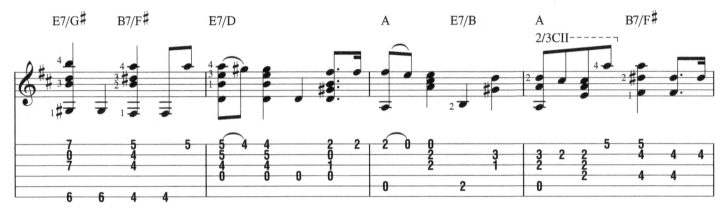

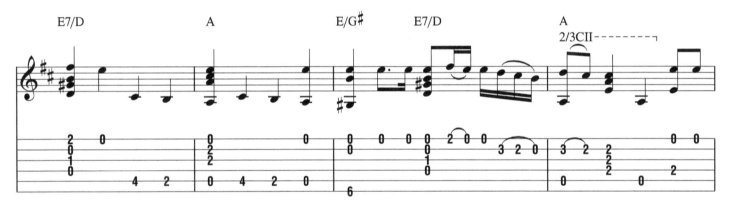

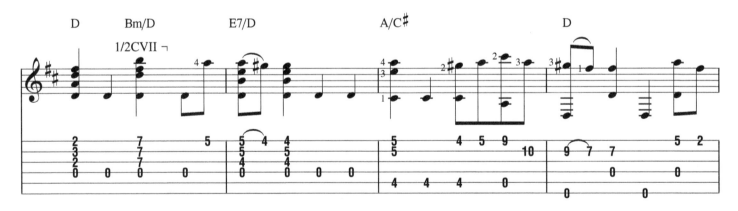

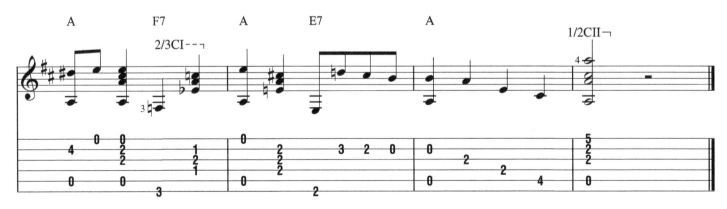

Bagatelle
Op. 119, No. 1
By Ludwig van Beethoven

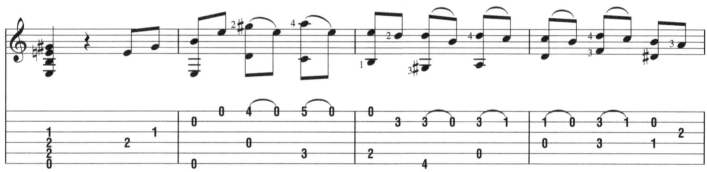

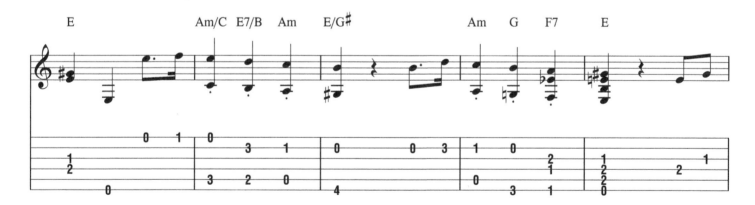

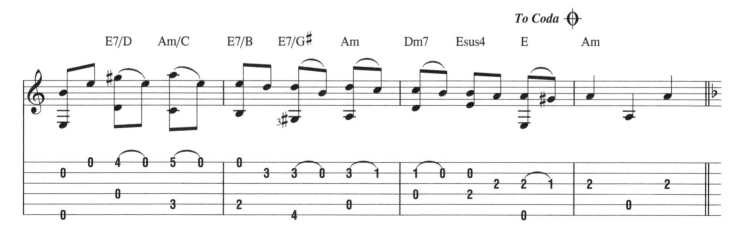

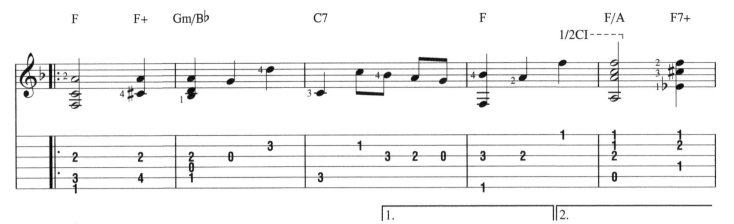

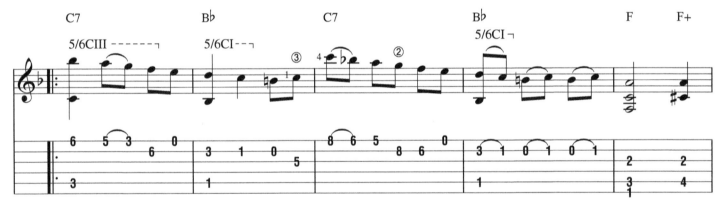

D.S. al Coda   **Coda**

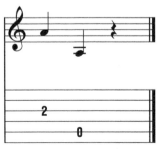

Für Elise

By Ludwig van Beethoven

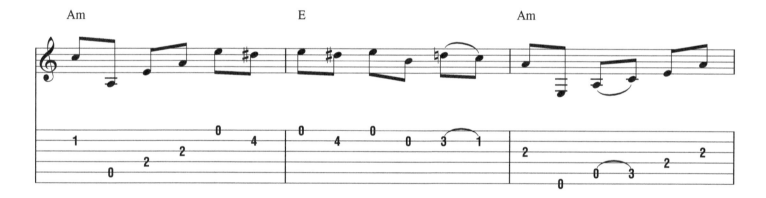

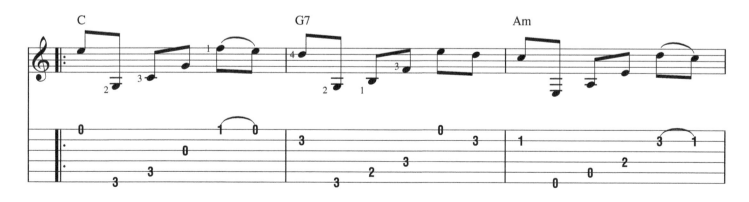

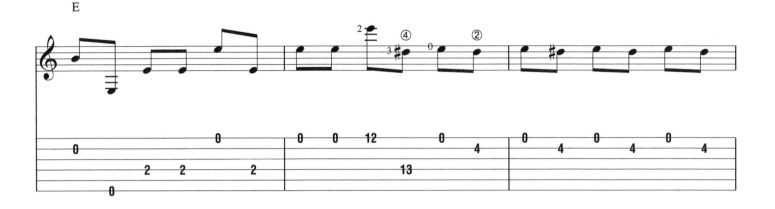

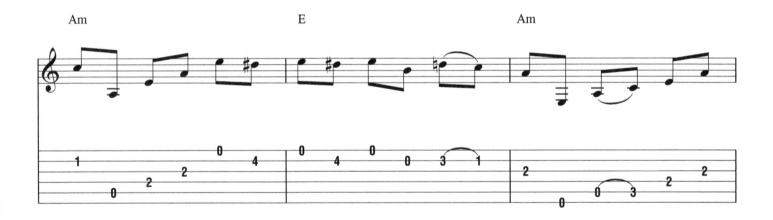

Minuet in G Major

By Ludwig van Beethoven

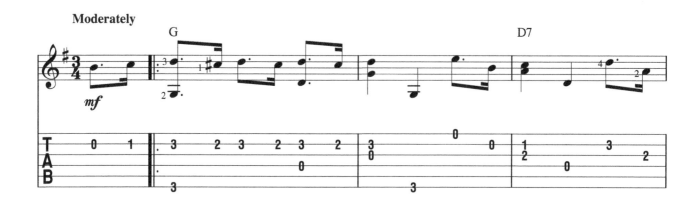

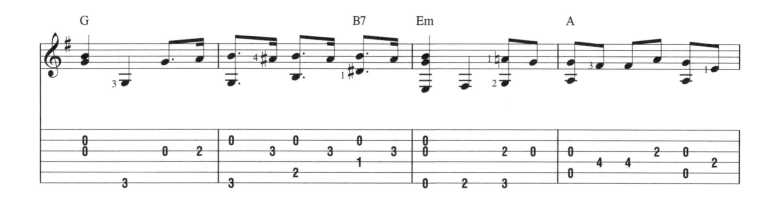

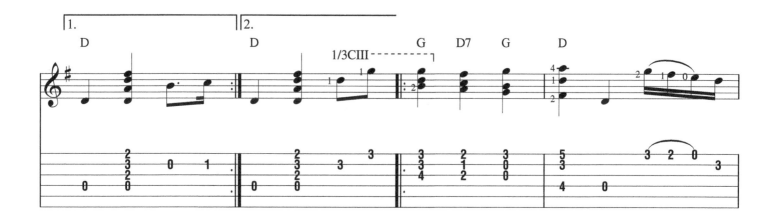

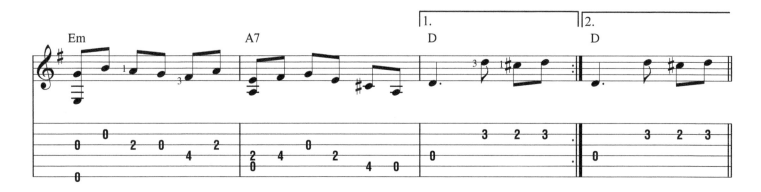

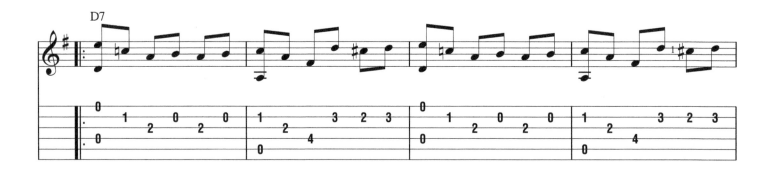

Piano Sonata No. 14 in C♯ Minor

("Moonlight")
Op. 27 No. 2 First Movement Theme
By Ludwig van Beethoven

Slowly

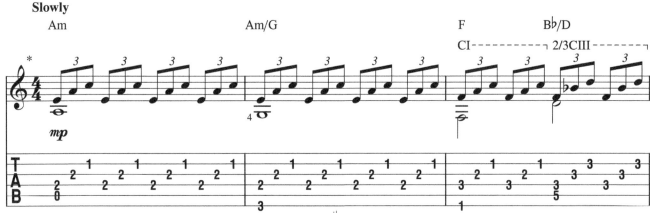

*This arrangement in A minor for playability. To play in C♯ minor, capo 4th fret.

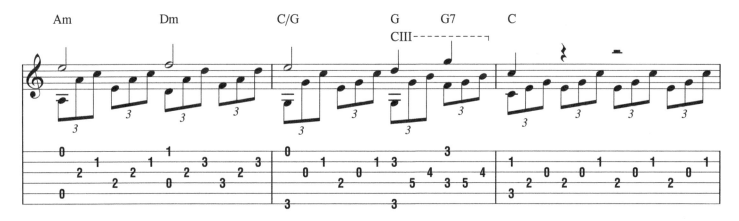

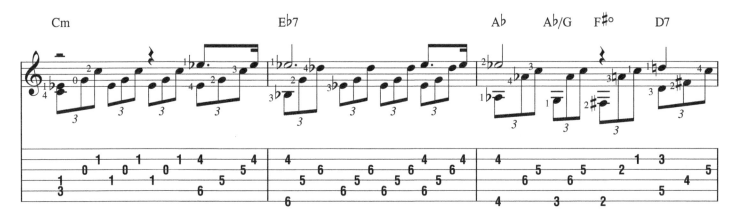

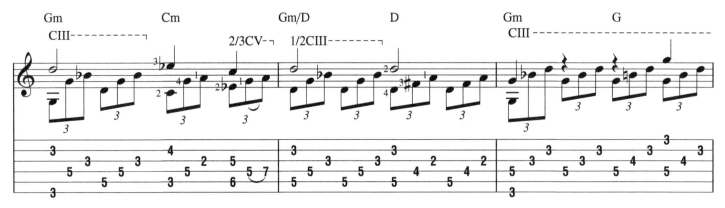

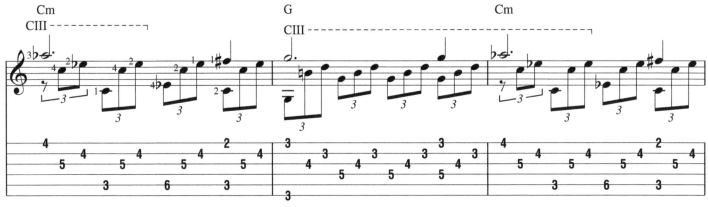

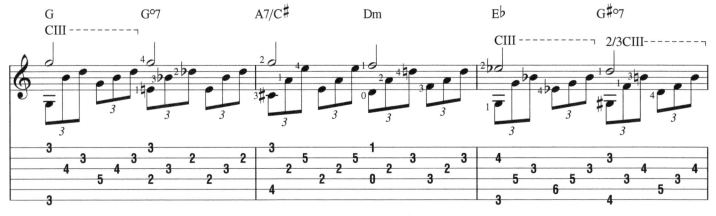

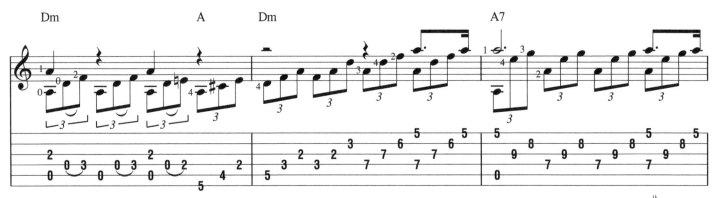

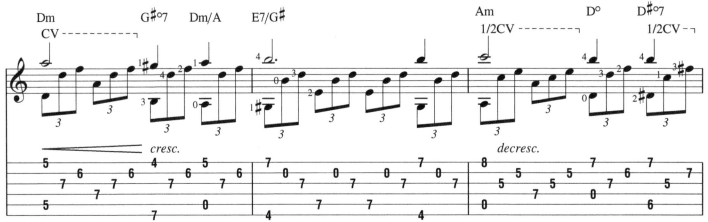

13

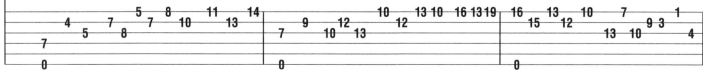

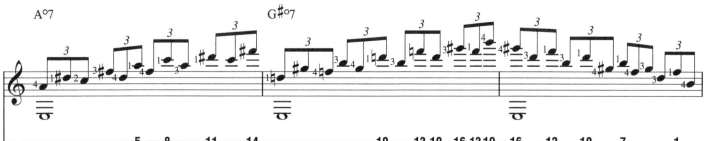

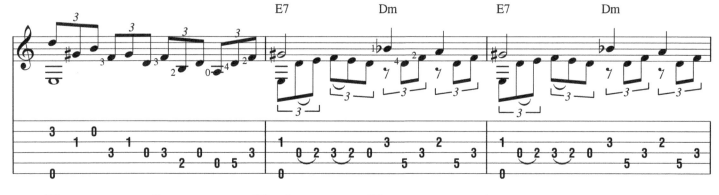

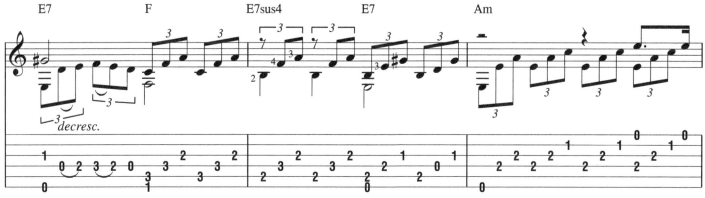

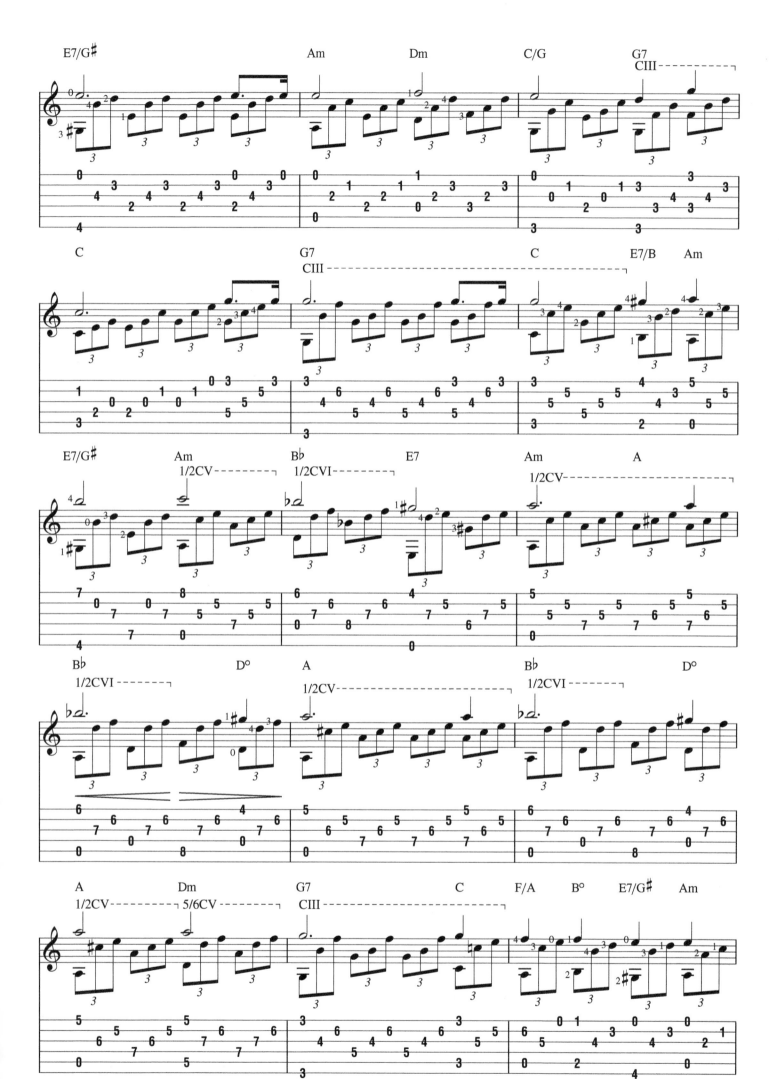

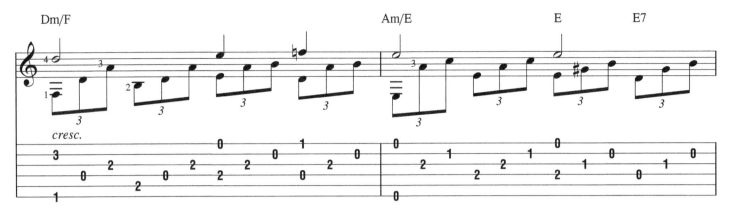

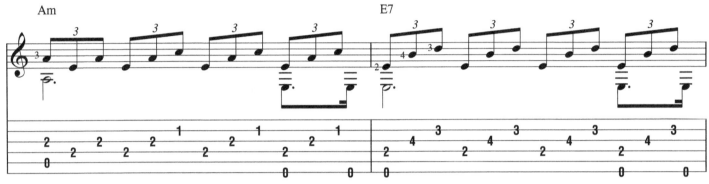

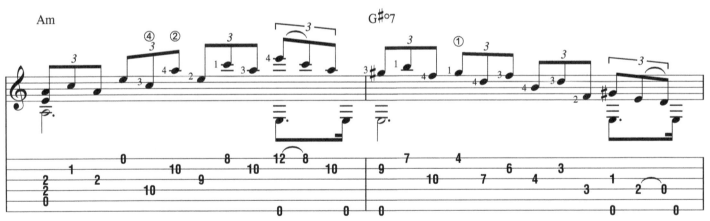

Ode to Joy

By Ludwig van Beethoven

Piano Concerto No. 5 in E-flat Major
("Emperor")
By Ludwig van Beethoven

Drop D tuning:
(low to high) D-A-D-G-B-E

Moderately fast

*This arrangement in D major for playability. To play in E♭ major, capo 1st fret.

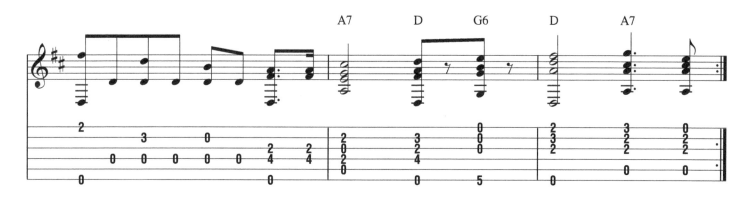

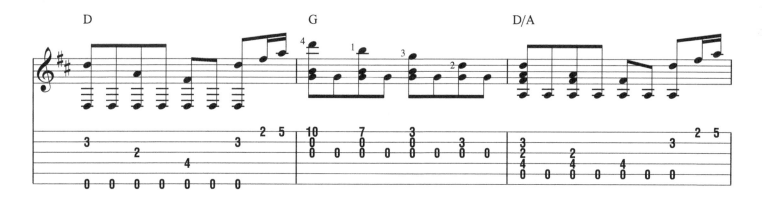

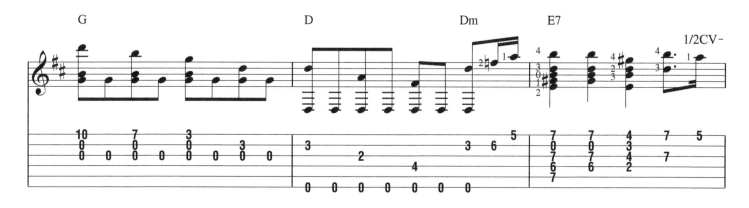

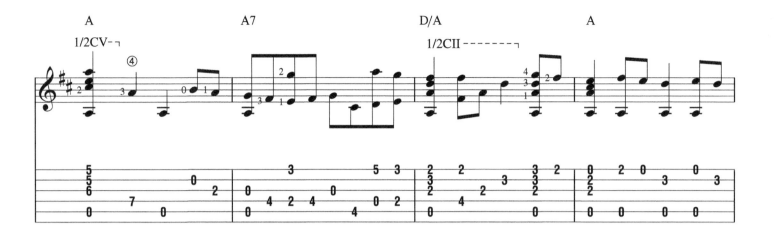

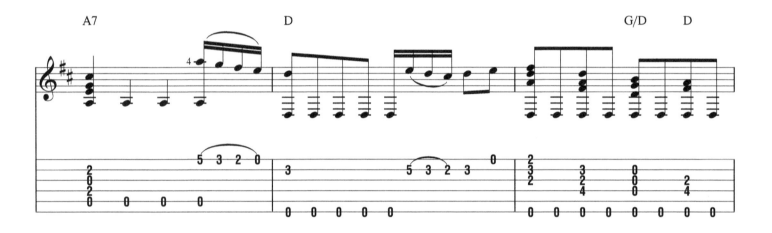

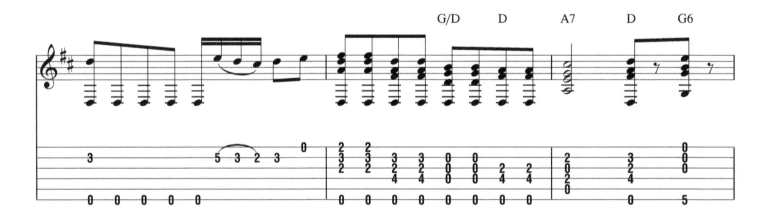

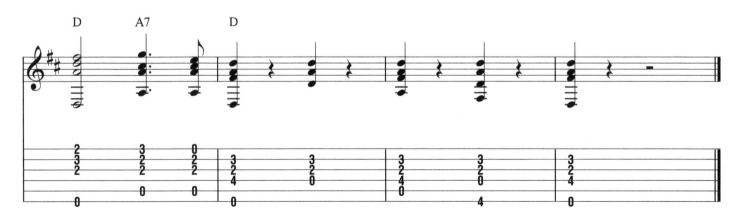

Piano Sonata No. 8, Op. 13

("Pathetique")
Second Movement Excerpt

By Ludwig van Beethoven

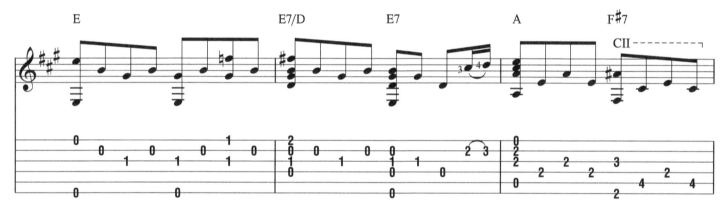

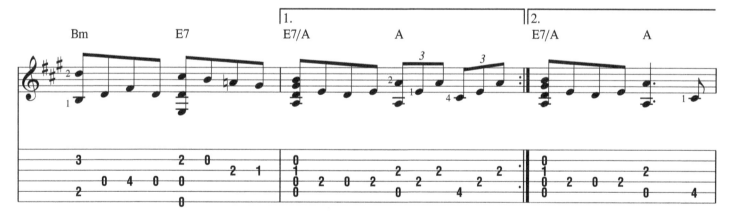

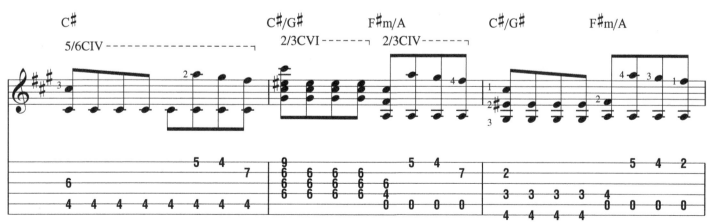

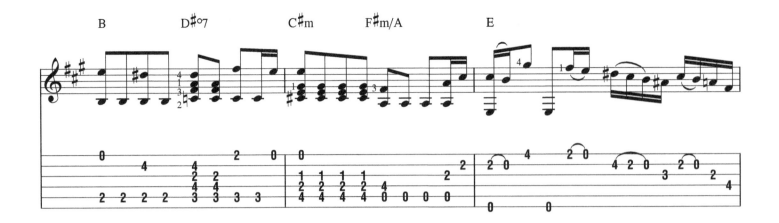

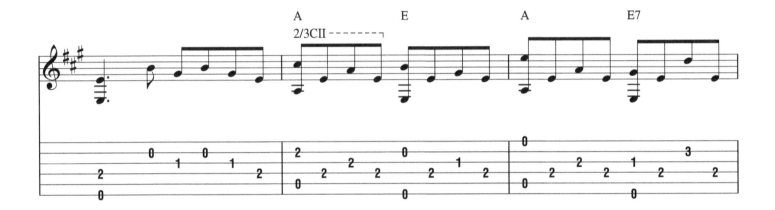

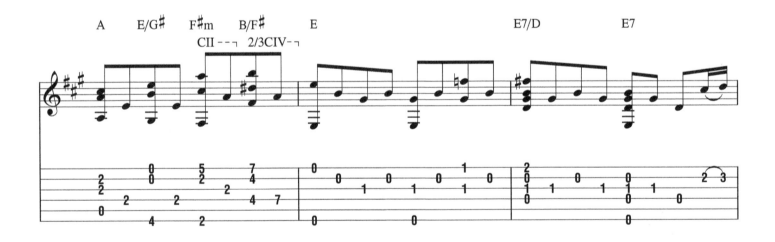

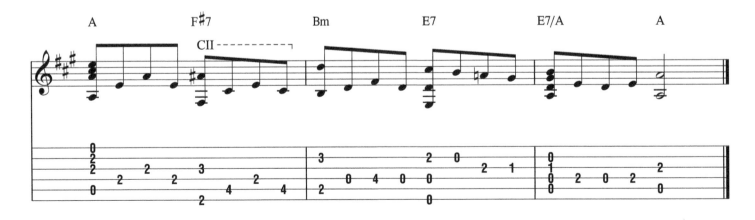

Piano Sonatina in G Major

By Ludwig van Beethoven

Moderately

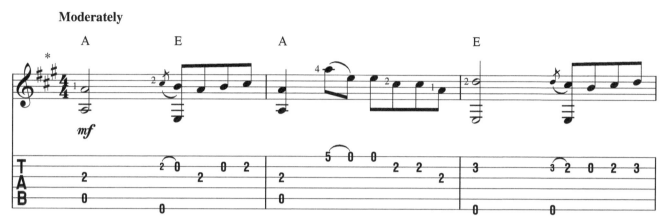

*This arrangement in A major for playability. To play in G major, tune down 1 step.

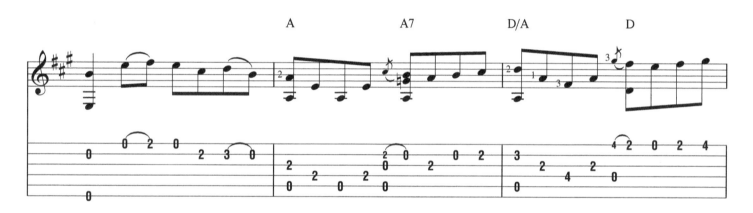

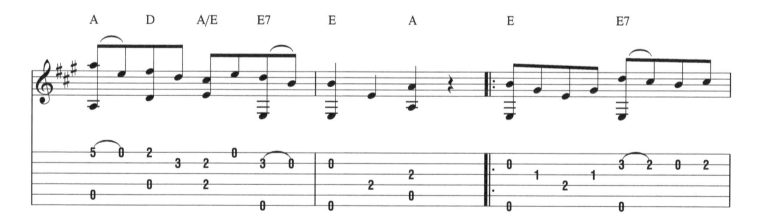

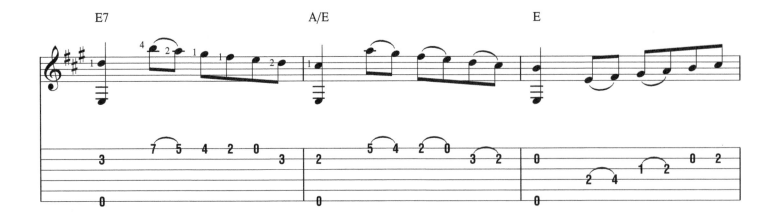

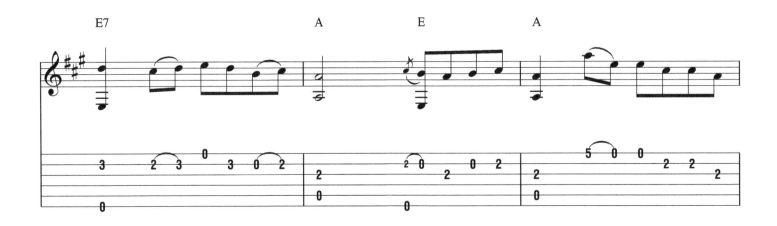

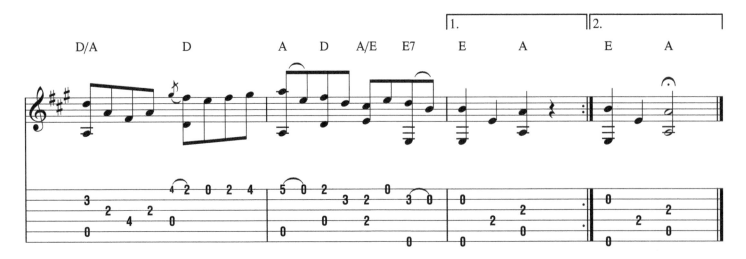

Symphony No. 3 in E-flat Major

("Eroica")

By Ludwig van Beethoven

Moderately fast

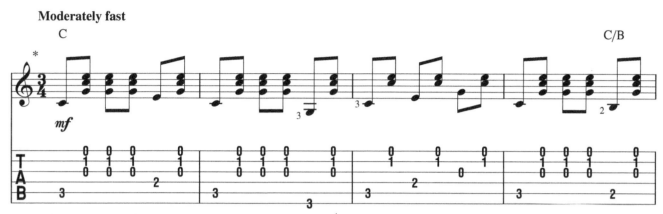

*This arrangement in C major for playability. To play in B♭ major, capo 3rd fret.

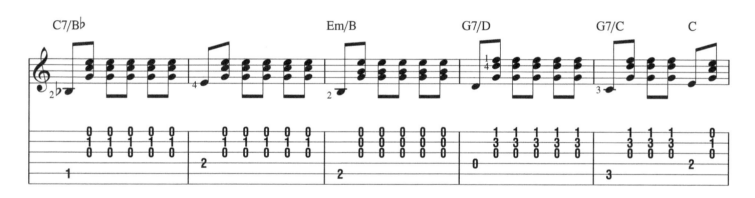

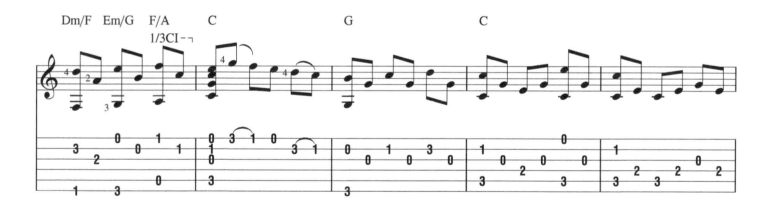

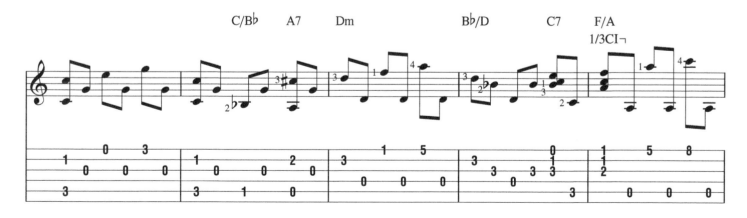

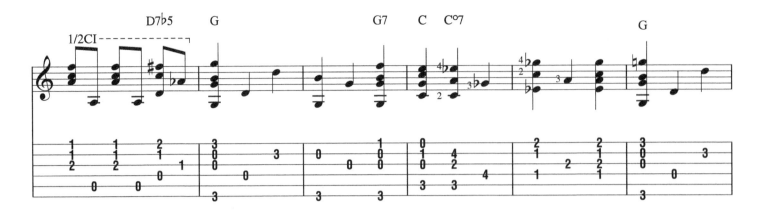

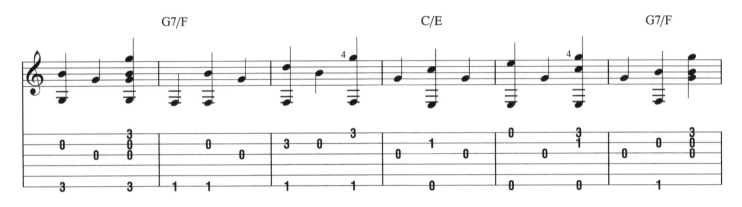

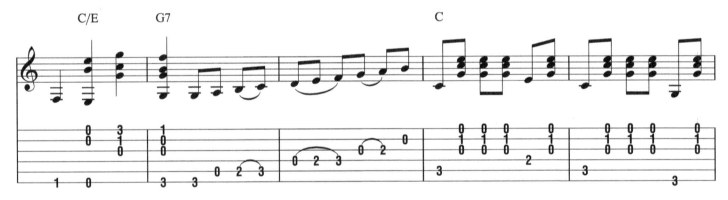

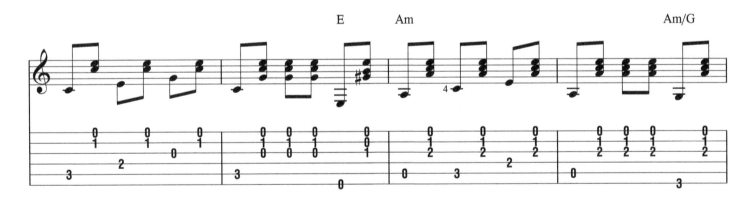

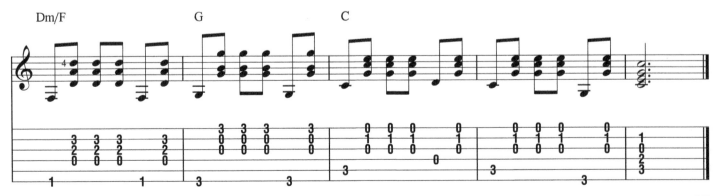

Symphony No. 6 in F Major
("Pastoral")
First Movement Excerpt
By Ludwig van Beethoven

Drop D tuning:
(low to high) D-A-D-G-B-E

Moderately

*This arrangement in D major for playability. To play in F major, capo 3rd fret.

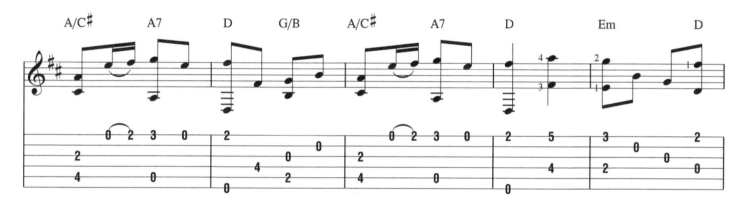

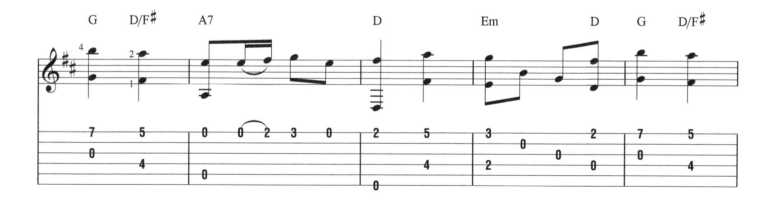

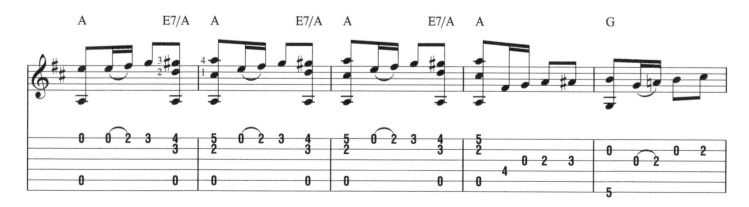

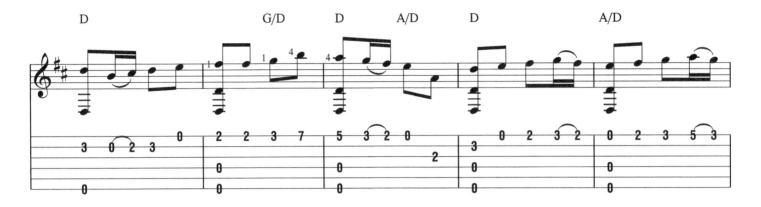

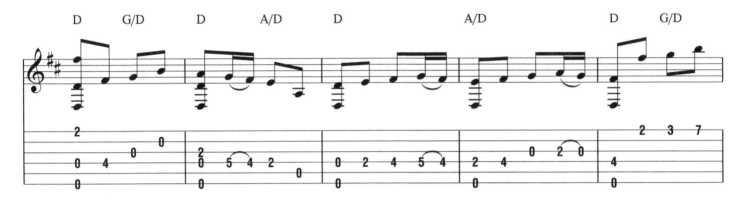

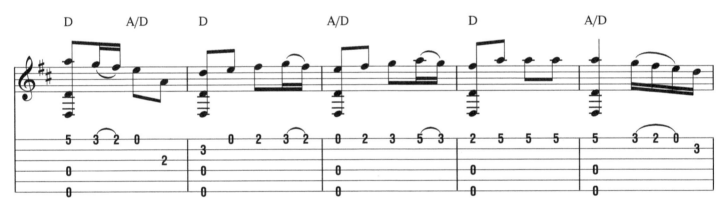

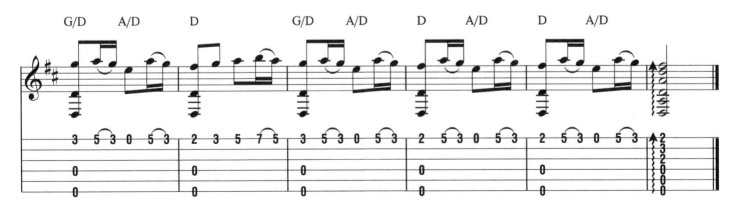

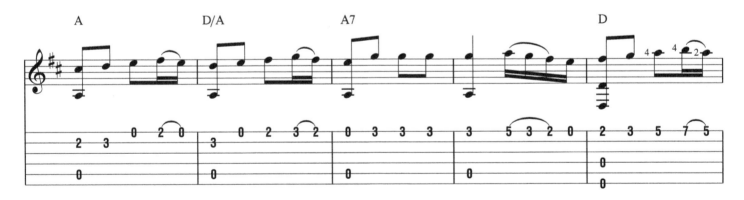

Symphony No. 7 in A Major
Second Movement (Allegretto)
By Ludwig van Beethoven

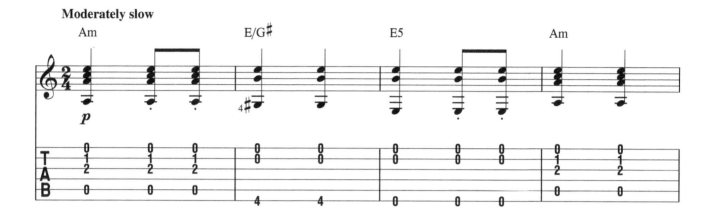

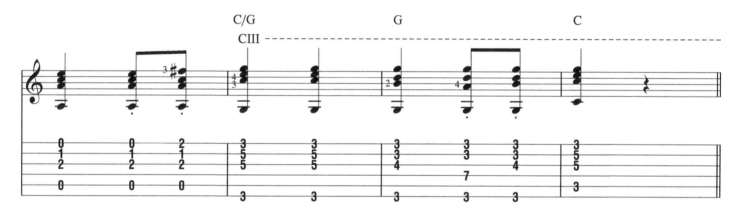

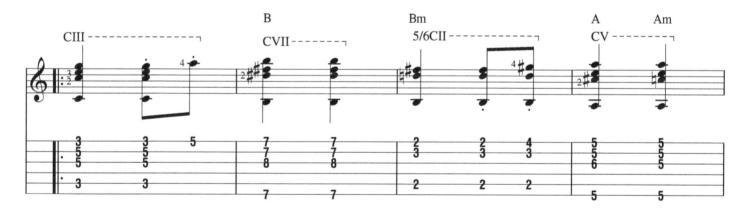

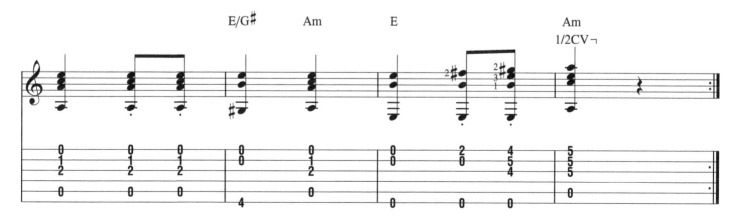

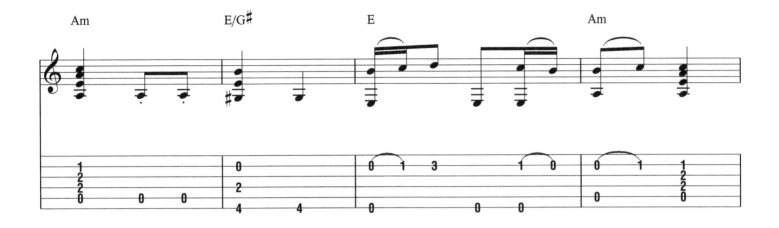

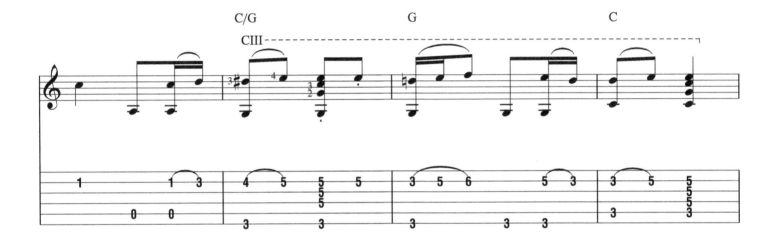

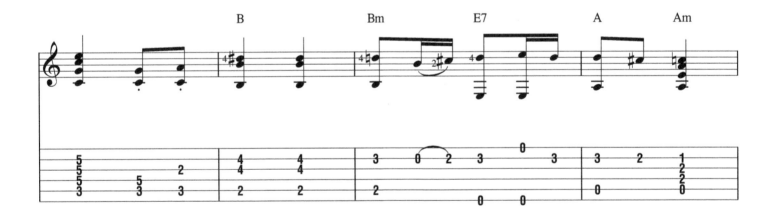

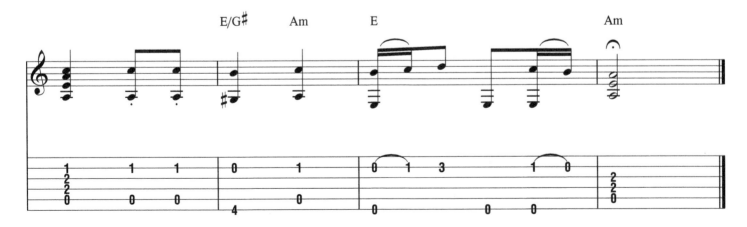

Symphony No. 5 in C Minor
First Movement Excerpt
By Ludwig van Beethoven

Drop D tuning:
(low to high) D-A-D-G-B-E

Fast

*This arrangement in D minor for playability. To play in C minor, tune down 1 step.

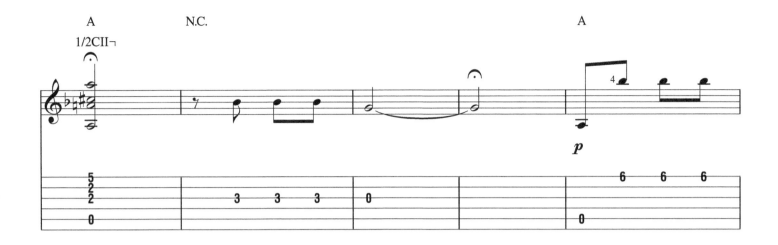

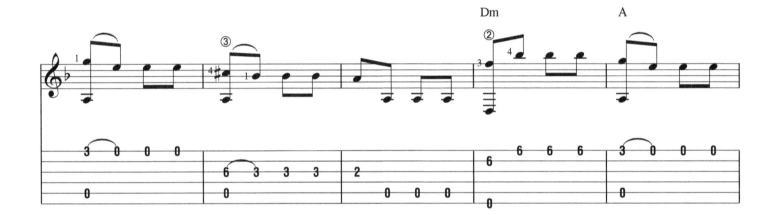

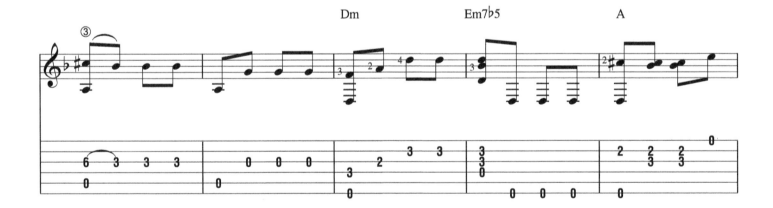

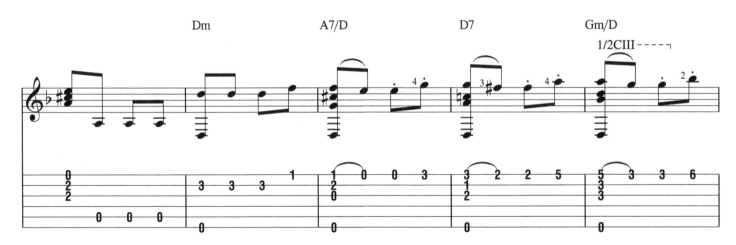

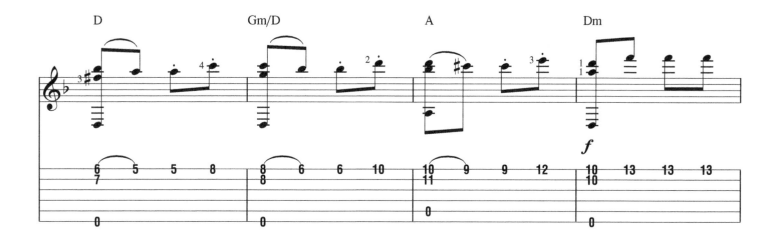

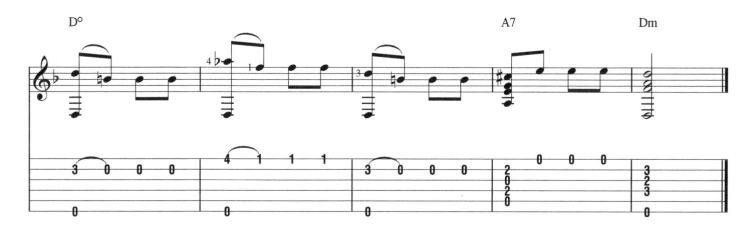

Turkish March
from THE RUINS OF ATHENS
By Ludwig van Beethoven

Drop D tuning:
(low to high) D-A-D-G-B-E

Moderately

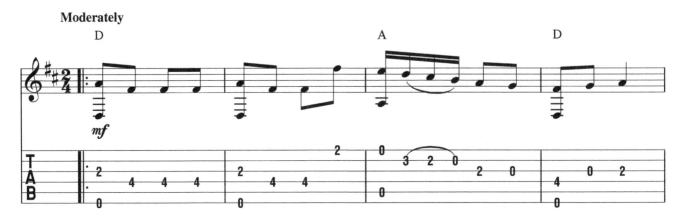

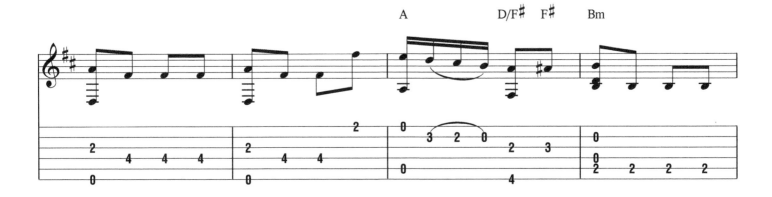

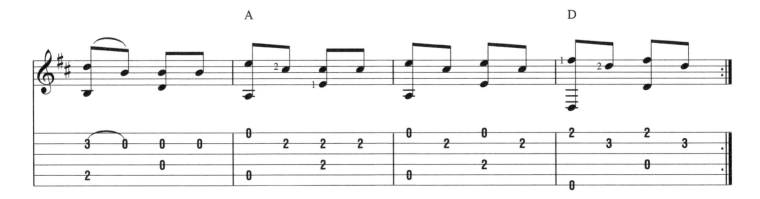

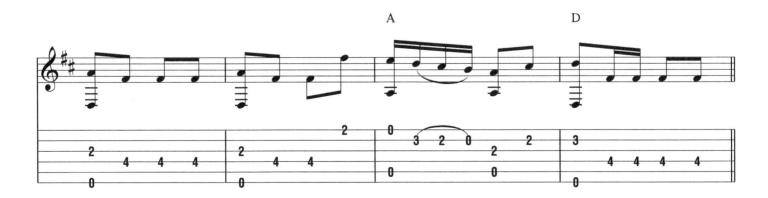

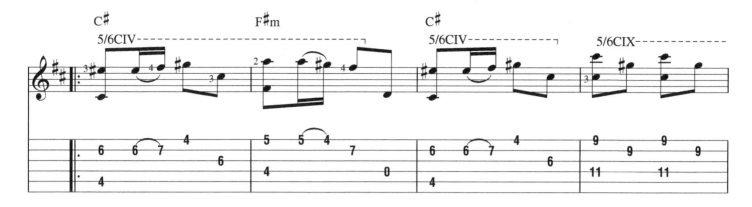

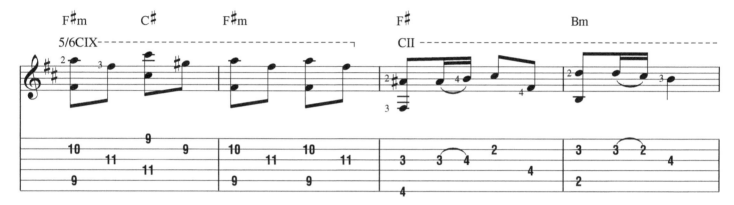

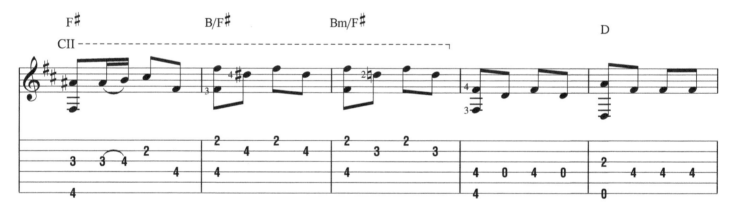

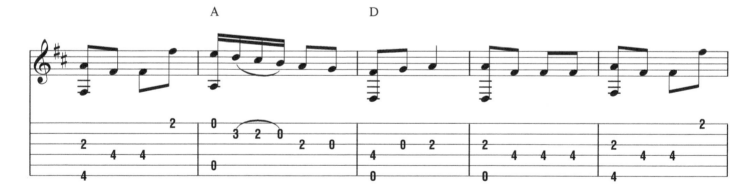

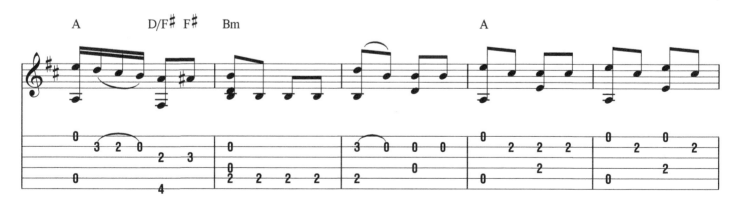

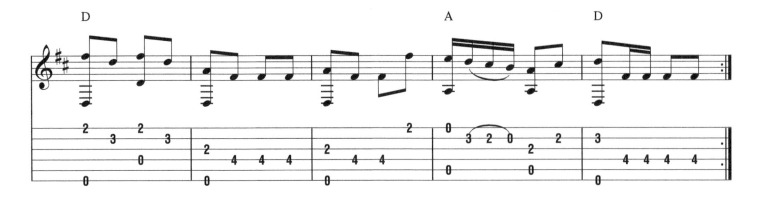

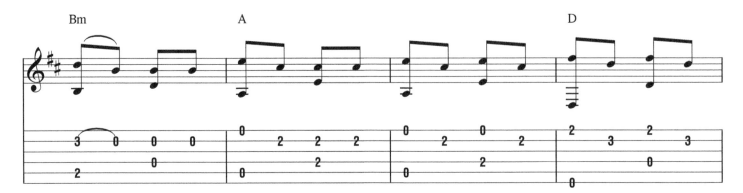

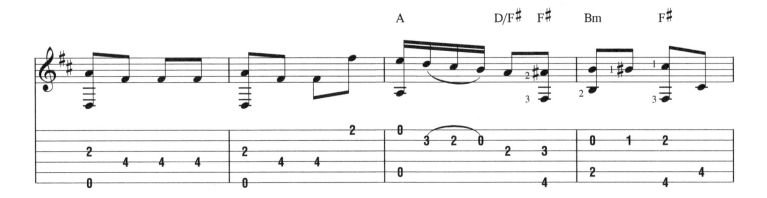

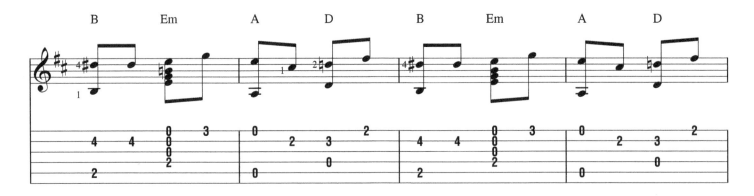

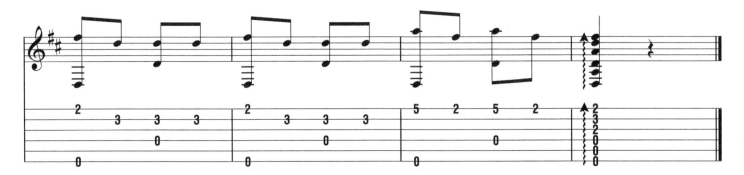

Violin Concerto in D Major

By Ludwig van Beethoven

Drop D tuning:
(low to high) D-A-D-G-B-E

Moderately

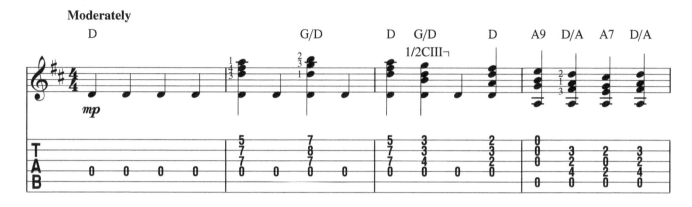

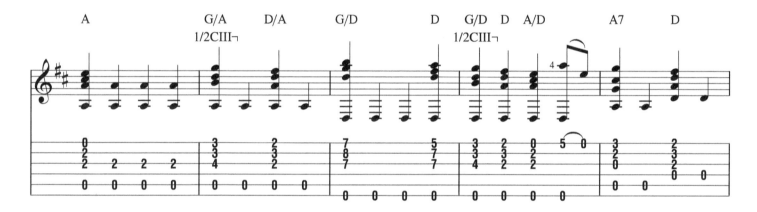

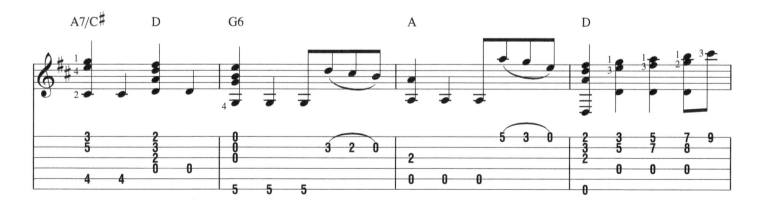

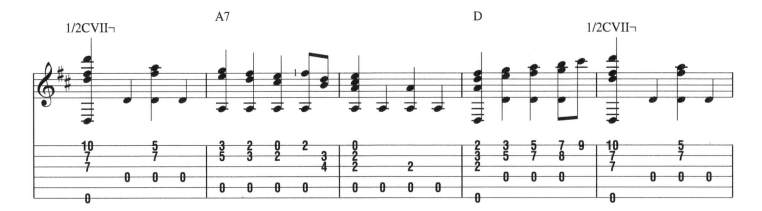

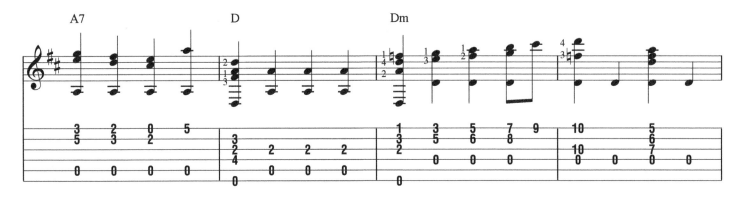

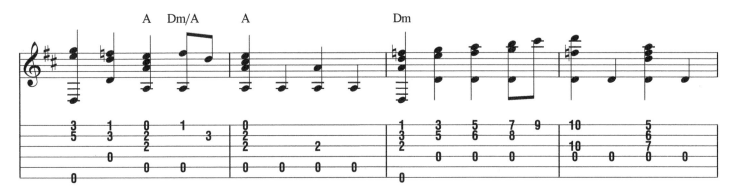

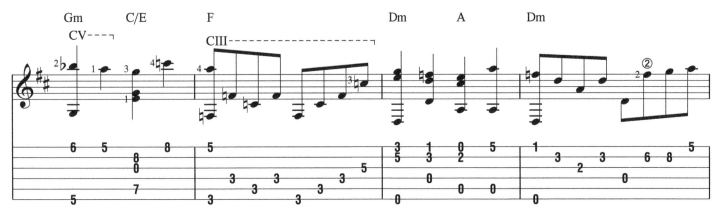

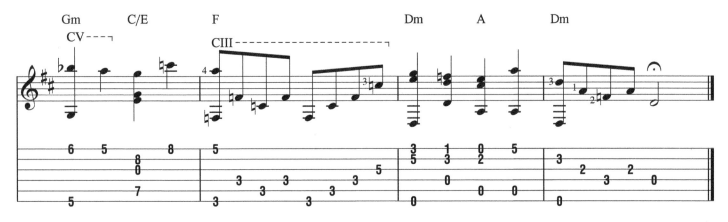

INTRODUCTION TO FINGERSTYLE GUITAR

Fingerstyle (a.k.a. fingerpicking) is a guitar technique that means you literally pick the strings with your right-hand fingers and thumb. This contrasts with the conventional technique of strumming and playing single notes with a pick (a.k.a. flatpicking). For fingerpicking, you can use any type of guitar: acoustic steel-string, nylon-string classical, or electric.

THE RIGHT HAND

The most common right-hand position is shown here.

Use a high wrist; arch your palm as if you were holding a ping-pong ball. Keep the thumb outside and away from the fingers, and let the fingers do the work rather than lifting your whole hand.

The thumb generally plucks the bottom strings with downstrokes on the left side of the thumb and thumbnail. The other fingers pluck the higher strings using upstrokes with the fleshy tip of the fingers and fingernails. The thumb and fingers should pluck one string per stroke and not brush over several strings.

Another picking option you may choose to use is called hybrid picking (a.k.a. plectrum-style fingerpicking). Here, the pick is usually held between the thumb and first finger, and the three remaining fingers are assigned to pluck the higher strings.

THE LEFT HAND

The left-hand fingers are numbered 1 through 4.

Be sure to keep your fingers arched, with each joint bent; if they flatten out across the strings, they will deaden the sound when you fingerpick. As a general rule, let the strings ring as long as possible when playing fingerstyle.

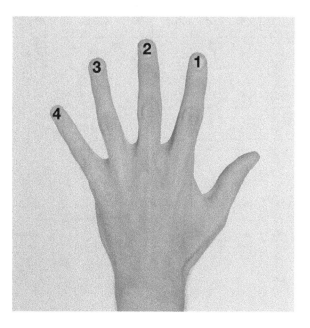

FINGERPICKING GUITAR BOOKS

Hone your fingerpicking skills with these great songbooks featuring solo guitar arrangements in standard notation and tablature. The arrangements in these books are carefully written for intermediate-level guitarists. Each song combines melody and harmony in one superb guitar fingerpicking arrangement. Each book also includes an introduction to basic fingerstyle guitar.

    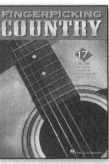 

Fingerpicking Acoustic
00699614 15 songs.....................$14.99

Fingerpicking Acoustic Classics
00160211 15 songs.....................$16.99

Fingerpicking Acoustic Hits
00160202 15 songs.....................$12.99

Fingerpicking Acoustic Rock
00699764 14 songs.....................$16.99

Fingerpicking Ballads
00699717 15 songs.....................$15.99

Fingerpicking Beatles
00699049 30 songs.....................$24.99

Fingerpicking Beethoven
00702390 15 pieces.....................$10.99

Fingerpicking Blues
00701277 15 songs.....................$12.99

Fingerpicking Broadway Favorites
00699843 15 songs.....................$9.99

Fingerpicking Broadway Hits
00699838 15 songs.....................$7.99

Fingerpicking Campfire
00275964 15 songs.....................$14.99

Fingerpicking Celtic Folk
00701148 15 songs.....................$12.99

Fingerpicking Children's Songs
00699712 15 songs.....................$9.99

Fingerpicking Christian
00701076 15 songs.....................$12.99

Fingerpicking Christmas
00699599 20 carols.....................$12.99

Fingerpicking Christmas Classics
00701695 15 songs.....................$7.99

Fingerpicking Christmas Songs
00171333 15 songs.....................$10.99

Fingerpicking Classical
00699620 15 pieces.....................$10.99

Fingerpicking Country
00699687 17 songs.....................$12.99

Fingerpicking Disney
00699711 15 songs.....................$17.99

Fingerpicking Early Jazz Standards
00276565 15 songs.....................$12.99

Fingerpicking Duke Ellington
00699845 15 songs.....................$9.99

Fingerpicking Enya
00701161 15 songs.....................$16.99

Fingerpicking Film Score Music
00160143 15 songs.....................$12.99

Fingerpicking Gospel
00701059 15 songs.....................$9.99

Fingerpicking Hit Songs
00160195 15 songs.....................$12.99

Fingerpicking Hymns
00699688 15 hymns.....................$12.99

Fingerpicking Irish Songs
00701965 15 songs.....................$10.99

Fingerpicking Italian Songs
00159778 15 songs.....................$12.99

Fingerpicking Jazz Favorites
00699844 15 songs.....................$12.99

Fingerpicking Jazz Standards
00699840 15 songs.....................$12.99

Fingerpicking Elton John
00237495 15 songs.....................$15.99

Fingerpicking Latin Favorites
00699842 15 songs.....................$12.99

Fingerpicking Latin Standards
00699837 15 songs.....................$17.99

Fingerpicking Andrew Lloyd Webber
00699839 14 songs.....................$16.99

Fingerpicking Love Songs
00699841 15 songs.....................$14.99

Fingerpicking Love Standards
00699836 15 songs.....................$9.99

Fingerpicking Lullabyes
00701276 16 songs.....................$9.99

Fingerpicking Movie Music
00699919 15 songs.....................$14.99

Fingerpicking Mozart
00699794 15 pieces.....................$10.99

Fingerpicking Pop
00699615 15 songs.....................$14.99

Fingerpicking Popular Hits
00139079 14 songs.....................$12.99

Fingerpicking Praise
00699714 15 songs.....................$14.99

Fingerpicking Rock
00699716 15 songs.....................$14.99

Fingerpicking Standards
00699613 17 songs.....................$15.99

Fingerpicking Wedding
00699637 15 songs.....................$10.99

Fingerpicking Worship
00700554 15 songs.....................$14.99

Fingerpicking Neil Young – Greatest Hits
00700134 16 songs.....................$17.99

Fingerpicking Yuletide
00699654 16 songs.....................$12.99

HAL•LEONARD®
Order these and more great publications from your favorite music retailer at
halleonard.com

Prices, contents and availability subject to change without notice.

CLASSICAL GUITAR

INSTRUCTIONAL BOOKS & METHODS AVAILABLE FROM HAL LEONARD

CLASSICAL STUDIES FOR PICK-STYLE GUITAR

by William Leavitt
Berklee Press

This Berklee Workshop, featuring over 20 solos and duets by Bach, Carcassi, Paganini, Sor and other renowned composers, is designed to acquaint intermediate to advanced pick-style guitarists with some of the excellent classical music that is adaptable to pick-style guitar. With study and practice, this workshop will increase a player's knowledge and proficiency on this formidable instrument.
50449440..$12.99

ÉTUDES SIMPLES FOR GUITAR

by Leo Brouwer
Editions Max Eschig

This new, completely revised and updated edition includes critical commentary and performance notes. Each study is accompanied by an introduction that illustrates its principal musical features and technical objectives, complete with suggestions and preparatory exercises.
50565810 Book/CD Pack........................$26.99

FIRST BOOK FOR THE GUITAR

by Frederick Noad
G. Schirmer, Inc.

A beginner's manual to the classical guitar. Uses a systematic approach using the interesting solo and duet music written by Noad, one of the world's foremost guitar educators. No musical knowledge is necessary. Student can progress by simple stages. Many of the exercises are designed for a teacher to play with the students. Will increase student's enthusiasm, therefore increasing the desire to take lessons.
50334370 Part 1.......................................$12.99
50334520 Part 2.......................................$17.99
50335160 Part 3.......................................$16.99
50336760 Complete Edition....................$32.99

HAL LEONARD CLASSICAL GUITAR METHOD

INCLUDES TAB

by Paul Henry

This comprehensive and easy-to-use beginner's guide uses the music of the master composers to teach you the basics of the classical style and technique. Includes pieces by Beethoven, Bach, Mozart, Schumann, Giuliani, Carcassi, Bathioli, Aguado, Tarrega, Purcell, and more. Includes all the basics plus info on PIMA technique, two- and three-part music, time signatures, key signatures, articulation, free stroke, rest stroke, composers, and much more.
00697376 Book/Online Audio (no tab).................$16.99
00142652 Book/Online Audio (with tab).............$17.99

A MODERN APPROACH TO CLASSICAL GUITAR

by Charles Duncan

This multi-volume method was developed to allow students to study the art of classical guitar within a new, more contemporary framework. For private, class or self-instruction.

00695114 Book 1 – Book Only..............................$8.99
00695113 Book 1 – Book/Online Audio................$12.99
00699204 Book 1 – Repertoire Book Only............$11.99
00699205 Book 1 – Repertoire Book/Online Audio.$16.99
00695116 Book 2 – Book Only..............................$7.99
00695115 Book 2 – Book/Online Audio................$12.99
00699208 Book 2 – Repertoire..............................$12.99
00699202 Book 3 – Book Only..............................$9.99
00695117 Book 3 – Book/Online Audio................$14.99
00695119 Composite Book/CD Pack.....................$32.99

100 GRADED CLASSICAL GUITAR STUDIES

Selected and Graded by Frederick Noad

Frederick Noad has selected 100 studies from the works of three outstanding composers of the classical period: Sor, Giuliani, and Carcassi. All these studies are invaluable for developing both right hand and left hand skills. Students and teachers will find this book invaluable for making technical progress. In addition, they will build a repertoire of some of the most melodious music ever written for the guitar.
14023154...$29.99

CHRISTOPHER PARKENING GUITAR METHOD

THE ART & TECHNIQUE OF THE CLASSICAL GUITAR

Guitarists will learn basic classical technique by playing over 50 beautiful classical pieces, 26 exercises and 14 duets, and through numerous photos and illustrations. The method covers: rudiments of classical technique, note reading and music theory, selection and care of guitars, strategies for effective practicing, and much more!
00696023 Book 1/Online Audio............................$22.99
00695228 Book 1 (No Audio)................................$14.99
00696024 Book 2/Online Audio............................$22.99
00695229 Book 2 (No Audio)................................$14.99

SOLO GUITAR PLAYING

by Frederick M. Noad

Solo Guitar Playing can teach even the person with no previous musical training how to progress from simple single-line melodies to mastery of the guitar as a solo instrument. Fully illustrated with diagrams, photographs, and over 200 musical exercises and repertoire selections, these books offer instruction in every phase of classical guitar playing.
14023147 Book 1/Online Audio............................$34.99
14023153 Book 1 (Book Only)..............................$24.99
14023151 Book 2 (Book Only)..............................$19.99

TWENTY STUDIES FOR THE GUITAR

ANDRÉS SEGOVIA EDITION

by Fernando Sor
Performed by Paul Henry

20 studies for the classical guitar written by Beethoven's contemporary, Fernando Sor, revised, edited and fingered by the great classical guitarist Andres Segovia. These essential repertoire pieces continue to be used by teachers and students to build solid classical technique. Features 50-minute demonstration audio.
00695012 Book/Online Audio..............................$22.99
00006363 Book Only...$9.99

HAL•LEONARD®

Order these and more publications from your favorite music retailer at
halleonard.com